EXPLORING THE SOLAR SYSTEM

SUN

GILES SPARROW

Heinemann Library
Chicago, Illinois

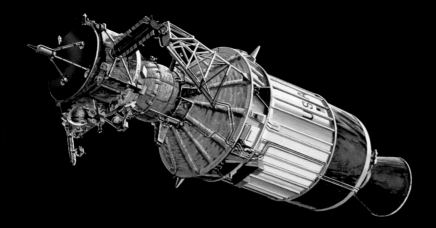

SUN

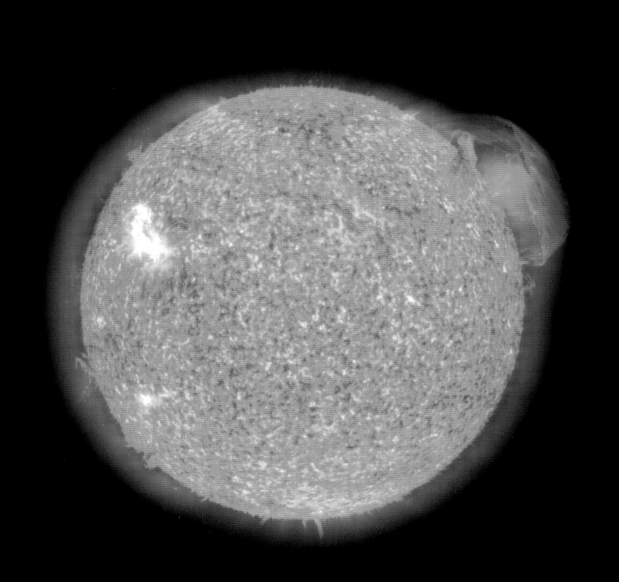

Published by Heinemann Library,
an imprint of Reed Educational & Professional Publishing,
100 N. LaSalle, Suite 300, Chicago, IL 60602
Customer Service 888-454-2279
Visit our website at www.heinemannlibrary.com

Produced by Brown Partworks
Project Editor: Ben Morgan
Deputy Editor: Sally McFall
Managing Editor: Anne O'Daly
Designer: Steve Wilson
Illustrator: Mark Walker
Picture Researcher: Helen Simm
Consultant: Peter Bond

© 2002 Brown Partworks Limited

Printed in Singapore

ISBN 1-57572-391-3 (hardback)   ISBN 1-58810-965-8 (paperback)
06 05 04 03 02 01   06 05 04 03 02 01
10 9 8 7 6 5 4 3 2 1   10 9 8 7 6 5 4 3 2 1

Library of Congress Cataloging-in-Publication Data

Sparrow, Giles.
  Sun / Giles Sparrow.
    p. cm. -- (Exploring the solar system)
Includes bibliographical references and index.
  1. Sun--Juvenile literature. [1. Sun.] I. Title. II. Series.
  QB521.5 .S77 2001
  523.7--dc21
                                        00-010443

BELOW: *The planets of the solar system, shown in order from the Sun:
Mercury, Venus, Earth, Mars, Jupiter, Saturn, Uranus, Neptune, Pluto.*

CONTENTS

Some words are shown in bold, like this.
You can find out what they mean by looking in the glossary.

Where Is the Sun?

The Sun is our nearest star. It lies at the center of our solar system, with all the planets, including Earth, in **orbit** around it. From Earth the Sun looks almost exactly the same size as the Moon, but this similarity is just a coincidence. The Sun is really 400 times wider than the Moon and 400 times further away.

The Sun is unimaginably vast, nearly 600 times bigger than all the planets put together. Because it is so huge, its **gravity** is enormous. Gravity is an invisible force that pulls objects together. Earth's gravity, for instance, makes objects fall to the ground. The Sun's gravity keeps all the planets moving in gigantic circles around it, called orbits.

The Sun is at the center of our solar system. Its enormous gravity keeps the nine planets orbiting around it.

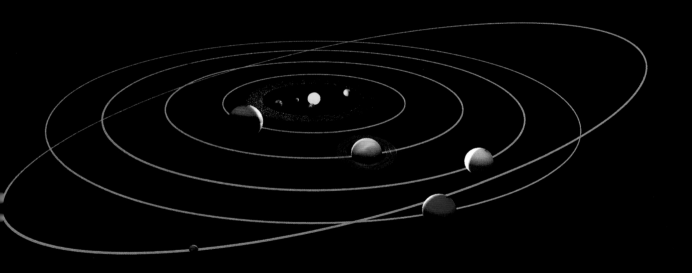

Distance from the planets

The diagram shows how far the Sun is from the planets that orbit around it. The furthest planets have the longest orbits. Pluto, for instance, takes 248 years to orbit the Sun.

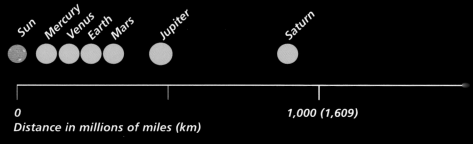

Sun Mercury Venus Earth Mars Jupiter Saturn

0 1,000 (1,609)

Distance in millions of miles (km)

Getting to the Sun

The time it takes to travel from Earth to the Sun depends on what type of transportation you use.

By car at 70 miles per hour (113 km per hour): 152 years

By rocket at 7 miles per second (11.2 km per second): 154 days

Time for light and radio signals from the Sun to reach Earth: 8 mins 20 sec

Size compared to Earth

Sun's diameter: 865,000 miles (1,392,000 km)

Earth's diameter: 7,926 miles (12,756 km)

The planets do not follow perfect circles as they orbit the Sun, but instead move though slightly oval shapes called **ellipses**. As a result, their distance from the Sun changes slightly. Earth lies at an average distance of 93 million miles (150 million kilometers) from the Sun, but the exact distance varies by around 3.2 million miles (5.1 million kilometers) during the year. The change in distance causes a very slight temperature change, but this has nothing to do with the seasons. In fact, Earth is furthest from the Sun when it is summer in the northern **hemisphere.**

Uranus

Neptune

Pluto

2,000 (3,219)

3,000 (4,828)

The View from Earth

Every day, the Sun rises over the eastern horizon, moves across the sky, and sets in the west. People once thought the Sun was moving around Earth, but it only appears to move because Earth is **rotating.**

Seen from the **equator,** the Sun always rises and sets at about the same times each day, and follows roughly the same path through the sky. However, in areas north or south of the equator the Sun's path through the sky depends on the time of year, or season. In these areas summers are warmer than winters because the Sun rises higher each day and spends a longer time in the sky.

Very occasionally, the Moon passes directly between the Sun and Earth, casting a shadow on Earth and blocking our view of the Sun. This event is called a solar **eclipse,** and it is the only chance we get to see the Sun's outer **atmosphere,** or **corona,** from Earth. When the glare of the main part of the Sun is hidden, we can see the wispy corona stretching away into space. Yet even during an eclipse the Sun is so bright that it is much too dangerous to look at directly, even through the darkest sunglasses.

Imagine you're about to join a **mission** to the Sun. Of course, it will be impossible to land on the Sun or look at it directly, but you will be able to get near enough to study the mysterious, stormy corona. With the aid of special cameras and colored filters you will even be able to look at the Sun's seething surface.

Seasons and the Sun

The seasons occur because Earth spins on a tilt. When the north pole is tilted toward the Sun, it is summer in the northern hemisphere and winter in the southern hemisphere. Likewise, when the south pole is tilted toward the Sun, it is summer in the southern hemisphere and winter in the northern hemisphere.

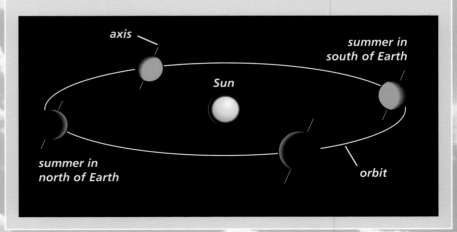

axis

summer in south of Earth

Sun

summer in north of Earth

orbit

Your trip will take several months, so your ship will need a large supply of fuel and food. You won't be able to travel there in a straight line because if you did, the Sun's immense **gravity** would trap your ship in a fatal collision course with the Sun. So instead, you take a long, curved path that will put your ship in **orbit** around the Sun.

Your ship, constructed in orbit around Earth, is equipped with thick shields to withstand the Sun's intense heat and **radiation.** Earth's atmosphere and **magnetic field** protect us from the full force of the Sun's radiation, but in outer space the Sun's rays can be deadly.

After weeks of preparation and training, you board the space shuttle that will ferry you to the waiting ship. As soon as you leave Earth's atmosphere the Sun becomes much easier to study. The air and dust in Earth's atmosphere cause a blinding glare around the Sun, making it impossible to see the Sun's outer layers. However, in space you can see the outer layers of the Sun simply by holding up a circular disk to cover the Sun's face. Once your eyes adjust, you can see the magnificent glowing halo that makes up the Sun's corona. You can also see strange arches of light rising into the corona. These are **prominences.** By projecting the Sun's light through a pinhole and onto a screen—a technique you can use on Earth too—you can even see features on the surface, such as dark patches called **sunspots.**

The Sun casts a brilliant fiery glow over the sea as it sinks slowly toward the horizon on Earth.

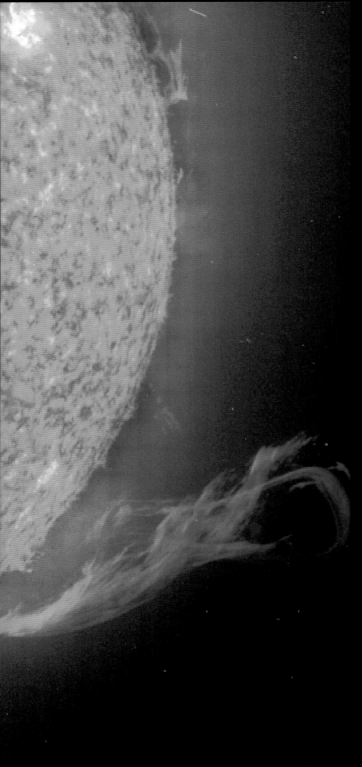

Into Orbit

After several months your ship goes into **orbit** above the Sun. Although the Sun looks like a ball of fire from Earth, your ship's instruments reveal that it is not made of fire but gas. The gas glows because it is incredibly hot.

Even though you are orbiting a million miles above the Sun's surface, you are still inside the **corona.** The corona is made of the same gas that makes up the Sun, but it is much less **dense.** An automatic scoop collects enough of the gas to analyze. The gas is hydrogen, but it is very different from ordinary hydrogen. The Sun's intense heat has torn the **atoms** apart and turned the hydrogen into a special type of gas called **plasma.** The plasma in the corona is a searing 1.8 million °F (1 million °C), but fortunately it is so spread out that the heat hardly affects your ship.

Your ship keeps shaking slightly. This is caused by the **solar wind,** a constant stream of **plasma** that blasts into space from the Sun at up to 2 million miles per hour (3 million kilometers per hour). The Sun loses a million tons of matter every second because of the solar wind, but it is so massive—about 2 billion billion billion tons—that it would take a very long time to shrink noticeably!

Suddenly, alarms go off all over your ship. You rush to a window and see a terrifying sight. A vast arch of plasma has burst from the surface of the Sun, and you're heading straight for it. It's too late to change course, so you brace yourself for a crash.

A glowing tongue of plasma erupts from the Sun's seething surface, extending hundreds of thousands of miles into space.

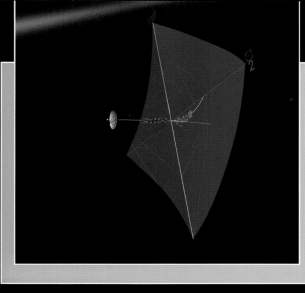

Riding the solar wind

*In the future, astronauts might use the solar wind to blow them across the solar system, just like sailors. But solar sailing would need sails much bigger than those on any ship. This is because although the solar wind is very fast, it is far less substantial than Earth's air. However, in **zero gravity**, solar sails of many square miles, like the one illustrated at left, might one day be possible.*

But the crash doesn't happen—your ship just passes right through the plasma cloud and moves on. Your instruments show that the outside temperature has suddenly dropped. The loop of gas was a **prominence.** These are actually much cooler than the gas in the corona.

The windows of your ship have special filters that let you look at the Sun's surface. You can't make out much detail, but you can see the dark **sunspots** that you saw with the pinhole camera. By recording the movement of the biggest sunspots over several days, you can measure how fast the Sun spins. At the **equator** it **rotates** once every 25 days, but there's something odd. The Sun's **poles** take ten days longer than the equator to rotate once. This strange rotation can only happen if the Sun is made of nothing but gas. Even the gas giant planets Jupiter and Saturn do not rotate as unevenly as this, because they have solid cores. But if the Sun is just a huge ball of gas, then why does it seem to have a definite surface? It's time to send down a probe and investigate the Sun's outer layers in more detail.

Vast loops of plasma, called prominences, rise from the Sun's surface into the corona. Although most of the plasma falls back to the surface, some of it blows out to space in the solar wind.

Sunscape

As you've discovered, the Sun is a violent and stormy place. In fact, the Sun goes through a regular eleven-year cycle of activity called the solar cycle, and you've arrived during the most violent part of the cycle. At this point in the solar cycle, the number of **sunspots** reaches a peak. You decide to launch your heavily shielded **space probe** away from the sunspots and toward a featureless area of the surface—it's best to find out about the quiet parts of the Sun before you look at the active regions.

As the probe drops through the **corona,** the temperature rises steadily and the gas gets **denser.** Then something strange starts to happen. A few thousand miles above the surface, the temperature actually drops from a million degrees to only a few thousand degrees, even though the **plasma** around the probe is getting much denser. Switching on filters that block out nearly all of the Sun's light, you point the probe's cameras straight down.

ABOVE: *The Sun's **atmosphere,** or corona, is full of stormy activity at the peak of the solar cycle.*

BELOW: *This photograph of the Sun's surface shows the speckled pattern called granulation. The photograph also shows a massive explosion of plasma, called an eruptive **prominence.***

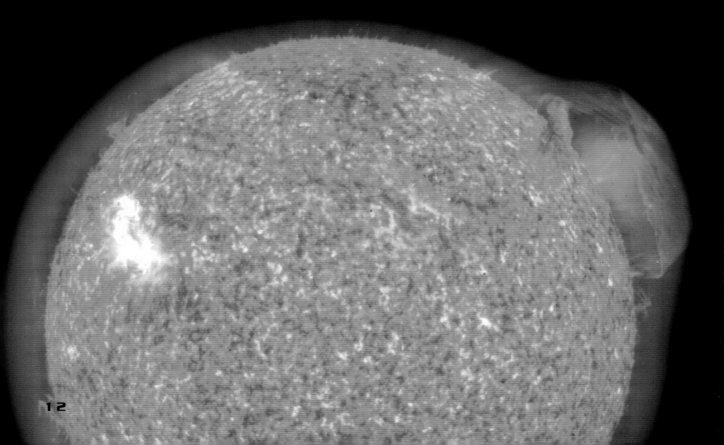

What you see surprises you. The surface is not featureless at all, but is seething with movement like a pan of boiling liquid. A pattern of bright and dark speckles, known as **granulation,** covers the surface. Each speckle is about 600 miles (1,000 kilometers) across. The speckles come and go as you watch, but the pattern stays the same. The probe registers the surface temperature as 9,900°F (5,500°C).

Something else strange is happening. Although the probe is falling, the Sun seems to be getting further away. From your orbit you see why: huge areas of the Sun are rising and falling, and the area below the probe is dropping away from it. It is almost as if the Sun were breathing. You turn the probe's camera to look across the solar surface, and you get another surprise: vast flames seem to be shooting into space. These "flames" are actually jets of plasma called **spicules.** Each is about 6,000 miles (10,000 kilometers) tall—the distance from Los Angeles to London. Spicules flicker and die in a matter of minutes. The plasma they shoot out of the Sun blows away in the **solar wind.**

ABOVE: *Fountains of plasma called spicules spurt up into the corona in this photograph of the Sun's south pole. Scientists think that spicules are an important source of the solar wind.*

Seeing the Sun in a different light

*Because the Sun is so bright, special filters are used to photograph it. Each type of filter reveals different features. In the photographs below, red light (left) shows the Sun's granulation, blue and **ultraviolet light** (center) shows the bands above and below the **equator** where sunspots appear, and greener light (right) enhances these bands even more. Although the Sun's surface looks solid in many photographs, this is just an illusion.*

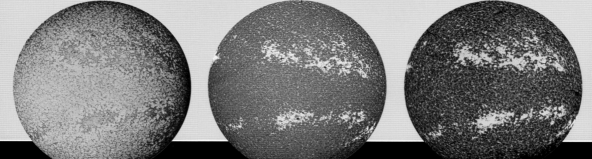

Sunspots

It's time to take another look at the more active areas of the Sun. Your **space probe** has burned up, so you decide to risk piloting your heavily shielded ship close to a cluster of **sunspots.**

ABOVE: *A cluster of sunspots forms a jagged line across the Sun's surface.*

Sunspots are the most obvious signs of solar activity. They often occur in clusters, and at the moment most seem to be near the Sun's **equator.** As you get close to one, you see that its dark center is surrounded by a slightly lighter area where hairlike rays spread out from the center. The whole spot is gigantic—big enough to swallow Earth. Your instruments tell you the temperature of the sunspot is a searing 6,300°F (3,500°C). The only reason the spot looks dark is because the surrounding area is even brighter and hotter.

BELOW: *A solar flare blasts out of the Sun's surface. Solar flares usually last only a few minutes, yet manage to release a vast amount of energy in the form of radiation and plasma.*

Your ship's magnetic sensors are now showing very high readings. This is because a powerful **magnetic field** is coming out of the sunspot, just like Earth's magnetic field comes out from the **poles.** The hairlike rays must be caused by the magnetism—they look just like the pattern iron filings make when scattered around a magnet.

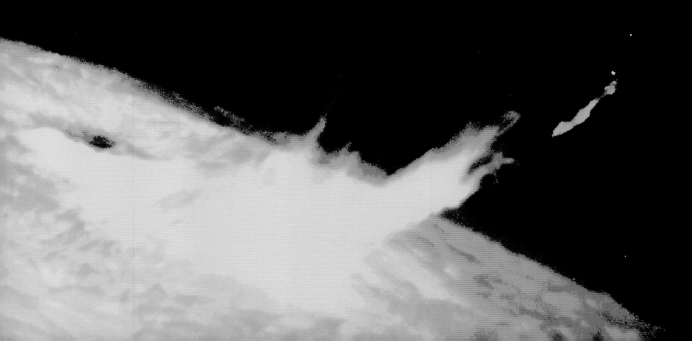

But magnetic poles come in pairs, so where is the other end of this magnetic field? You fly up and try to follow the direction of the field. It loops high into the **corona** before sinking down over another nearby sunspot.

Suddenly your ship's magnetic sensors go haywire—the field between the sunspots is shifting, changing, and shortening. You quickly decide to move your ship away and watch from a safe distance. The magnetic field continues to move as it rearranges itself, and as it does so it heats up the base of the corona. Then, with a blinding flash, a jet of plasma shoots out from above the sunspots and bursts through the corona as a small **solar flare.** The ship's detectors record bursts of high-energy **ultraviolet light** and **X-rays,** as well as brilliant visible light. Solar flares fling sudden bursts of plasma into the **solar wind.** When these reach Earth they produce shimmering lights, or **auroras,** at Earth's poles.

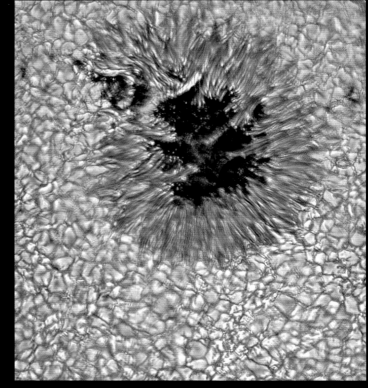

ABOVE: *This close-up of a sunspot shows the dark center surrounded by an area that looks like strands of hair or iron filings around a magnet. The granules on the Sun's surface, which are about 600 miles (1,000 km) across, are also clearly visible.*

The butterfly diagram

In the 1890s the British astronomer Edward Maunder (1851–1928) began keeping a daily record of sunspots. He plotted the results on a graph, showing how sunspot positions alter over time. Astronomers still collect and plot this information today, and the result is a butterfly diagram (below). The diagram shows how the eleven-year solar cycle starts with a few sunspots far from the equator, and how sunspots form closer to the equator in ever greater numbers. Finally they disappear and the cycle begins again.

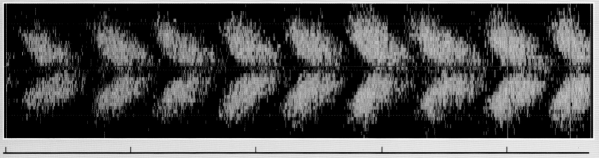

| 1900 | 1920 | 1940 | 1960 | 1980 |

Inside the Sun

This artist's impression shows the different layers inside the Sun. All the Sun's energy comes from the core, where the temperature soars to an amazing 27 million °F (15 million °C). Energy from the core takes 100,000 years to escape from the Sun as light.

Using the information from your **space probes,** and images of the Sun in different **wavelengths** of light, you can now start to piece together a complete picture of the Sun. Like most stars, the Sun is made of hydrogen, the gas you detected in the **corona.** Intense heat has broken apart the hydrogen **atoms** to form a special form of gas called **plasma.** Your probe also found evidence of other **elements,** including helium, sodium, and calcium.

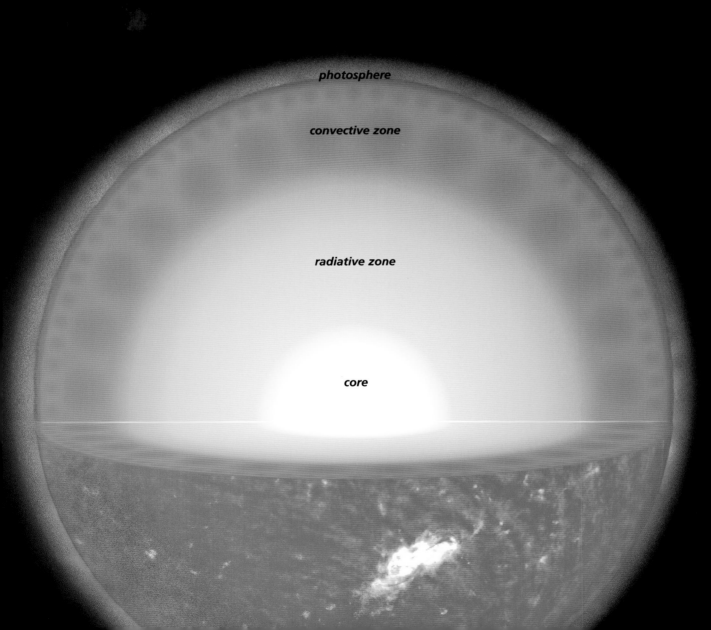

photosphere

convective zone

radiative zone

core

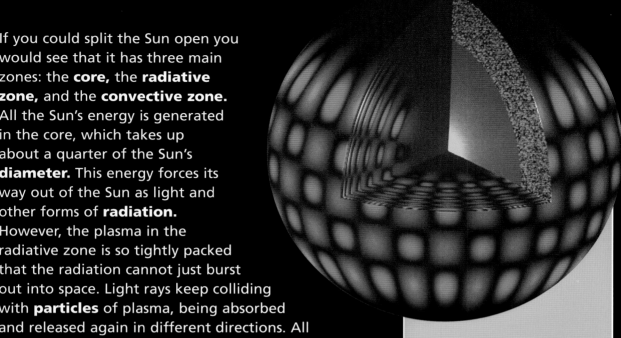

If you could split the Sun open you would see that it has three main zones: the **core,** the **radiative zone,** and the **convective zone.** All the Sun's energy is generated in the core, which takes up about a quarter of the Sun's **diameter.** This energy forces its way out of the Sun as light and other forms of **radiation.** However, the plasma in the radiative zone is so tightly packed that the radiation cannot just burst out into space. Light rays keep colliding with **particles** of plasma, being absorbed and released again in different directions. All this bouncing back and forth means that the radiation takes more than 100,000 years to work its way out through the radiative zone, steadily losing energy as it goes.

At the top of the radiative zone the plasma becomes opaque, which means that light from inside the Sun cannot shine through it. This layer of opaque plasma absorbs all the light from below and heats up rapidly. When gases heat up they rise—a process called convection. The hot plasma rises up through the convective zone until it reaches the Sun's surface— the **photosphere.** The photosphere is transparent, so sunlight flies through it and off into space. When the plasma has released its energy in sunlight, it cools down and sinks back to absorb more energy from below.

The areas of rising plasma in the convective zone are called convection cells. The granules you saw at the surface were the tops of convection cells. Their bright centers and dark edges show the hot gas rising in the middle of each cell and cooler gas sinking at the edges. It takes just ten days for energy from the core to pass through the convective zone. Sunlight released into space then takes just over eight minutes to reach Earth.

Sun sounds

Astronomers can learn about what's inside the Sun by studying how sound waves pass through it. Sound waves are produced by sunquakes—huge upheavals of the Sun's surface. The speed at which the sound waves travel depends on the thickness of the plasma the waves are moving through. Studies of sunquakes have revealed a distinct boundary between the radiative and convective zones—the radiative zone is calm and spins like a solid object, but the convection zone is as turbulent as a pan of boiling water. The image above shows one of the many different patterns that sound waves make as they pass through the Sun.

How the Sun Shines

Because the Sun is so massive, its **gravity** is enormous. As a result, the **plasma** in the **core** is squeezed into an extremely tight space, making it phenomenally **dense** and hot. The heat and pressure are so intense that they trigger a complex process called **nuclear fusion.** Scientists think that all the light that pours out of the Sun is created in the core by this process.

Throughout the Sun, **atoms** of **hydrogen** are broken apart into plasma. A hydrogen atom normally has two parts: a positively charged **particle** called a **proton,** which forms the center, or **nucleus,** of the atom, and a negatively charged particle called an **electron,** which flies around the proton.

Opposite charges attract, so electrons and protons normally stay together. However, when hydrogen gets very hot, the protons and electrons move apart and form plasma.

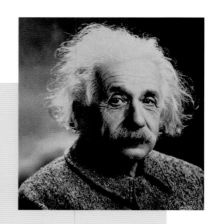

Einstein's theory

*Albert Einstein (1879–1955) was one of the greatest scientists of the 20th century. His famous Theory of Relativity, based on the equation $E = mc^2$, explains why nuclear fusion produces so much energy. When protons fuse together in the Sun, they lose a tiny amount of **mass,** and this mass turns into energy. According to the equation, the energy (E) equals the mass (m) times the speed of light squared (c^2). Because the speed of light squared is an amazingly huge number, a small amount of mass can turn into a vast quantity of energy. Every second, the Sun turns 4 million tons of its mass into pure energy by nuclear fusion.*

Nuclear fusion happens when pairs of protons fuse together. One of each pair loses a tiny amount of mass which turns into light energy (blue flash) and releases a particle called a neutrino. The proton is then a neutron. Each proton-neutron pair fuses with another proton, releasing yet more energy. Finally, triple particles fuse to form nuclei of helium atoms, releasing heat energy (yellow flash) and protons.

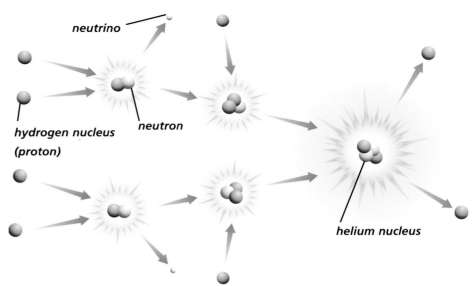

neutrino

hydrogen nucleus
(proton)

neutron

helium nucleus

In the Sun's core, protons fly around wildly and smash into each other. Positively charged objects normally repel each other, but protons in the core collide with such force that they sometimes fuse (join) together. This is nuclear fusion. It releases vast amounts of energy and also produces a new **element—helium.**

A hydrogen atom has just one proton in its nucleus, but helium has two protons and two particles called **neutrons.** So where do the neutrons come from? When a pair of protons fuse, one of them loses a tiny amount of mass. The lost mass turns into pure energy, and the proton becomes a neutron. This transformation also releases strange particles called **neutrinos,** which fly out into space and pass through anything in their path, including Earth. Astronomers have recently managed to detect neutrinos from the Sun, so the nuclear fusion theory is probably right.

LEFT: *Hydrogen bombs are powered by nuclear fusion, the same process that fuels the Sun.*

The neutrino mystery
Scientists at the Gran Sasso Laboratory in Italy (above) detected neutrinos from the Sun by using huge tanks of liquid buried deep underground to trap them. At first they thought their ideas about the Sun's energy source were proved right. However, they found only a third of the neutrinos needed to prove the theory. The neutrino problem is one of the Sun's biggest remaining mysteries.

The Solar Cycle

Astronomers have long wondered why the Sun's surface is so violently active, and why this activity follows an eleven-year cycle. A big clue to these puzzles comes from the strong **magnetic fields** that you discovered between pairs of **sunspots.**

Astronomers think that each solar cycle begins with a new magnetic field forming deep below the Sun's surface, at the boundary of the **radiative zone** and **convective zone.** Beneath the boundary, the inner part of the Sun spins at a constant rate, as if it were solid. But the convective zone spins unevenly, moving fastest at the **equator.** As the cycle progresses, the uneven movement of the convective zone stretches the magnetic field out of shape, pushing loops of magnetism out of the Sun's surface. Where they pass in and out, they create cooler patches—sunspots.

ABOVE: *These images shows solar activity over a two-year period. The first shows little activity. The second shows sunspots and prominences, which are common at the peak of the solar cycle.*

Let's twist again

When a solar cycle begins, a new magnetic field (1) forms in the Sun, running between the **poles.** *Because the Sun spins faster at the equator, the magnetic field gets twisted out of shape (2) and loops of magnetism begin to form (3). The loops get larger and more twisted (4), causing the* **corona** *to become stormy and turbulent as the cycle progresses.*

1
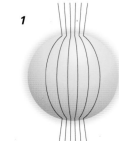

2

3

4

Later in the solar cycle the magnetic field gets even more twisted and more loops push their way to the surface. As time passes, the sunspots get ever closer to the equator. Halfway through the cycle, sunspot numbers reach a maximum. But they are now so close to the equator that they begin to cancel each other out, and the number starts to fall. After eleven years there are no sunspots left, and the Sun's magnetic field briefly disappears. Finally, a new magnetic field forms, but this one runs in the opposite direction—so the magnetic north and south poles of the Sun switch every eleven years!

The solar cycle doesn't just affect sunspots. The turbulent magnetic field can also cause flares, **prominences,** bursts of radio waves, and gigantic eruptions in the corona, known as **coronal mass ejections.**

The Little Ice Age

When astronomers began to research sunspot records during the 1800s they made a strange discovery. Between 1645 and 1715 there were almost no sunspots, as if the solar cycle had stopped. This period, called the Maunder minimum, may be linked to a series of very cold winters that Earth experienced at the time, known as the Little Ice Age. Many rivers froze over during the harsh weather, and Londoners held "frost fairs" on the Thames River, like the one shown in this painting from 1684. The Thames hasn't frozen over for centuries.

How the Sun Formed

The Sun is just one of around 200 billion stars that make up the Milky Way **galaxy.** Stars are dying and forming throughout the Milky Way, recycling the same material over and over. Our Sun's origins lie billions of years in the past, when a massive star blew itself apart in a gigantic explosion called a **supernova.** This violent death created all the elements that were to form the solar system, including the **atoms** in our own bodies.

The Sun is one of hundreds of billions of stars that make up the Milky Way. The Milky Way is a spiral galaxy, like the galaxy NGC1232 (below).

Supernovas happen when very large stars run out of fuel and die. When a large star reaches the end of its life, it no longer has enough energy to resist the tremendous force of its own **gravity.** The result is a sudden and violent death—the star's **core** collapses and crushes itself in seconds. The collapse causes a blast wave that flings the star's outer layers into space in a supernova explosion. For a short time, a supernova can shine as brightly as a galaxy.

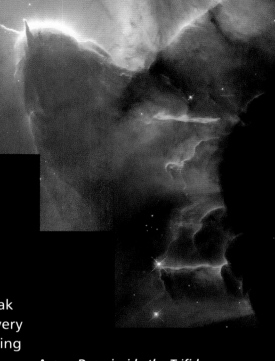

The **debris** from dead stars produces clouds of gas and dust called **nebulas,** and these are among the most beautiful objects in the universe. Nebulas have very weak gravity because the material inside them is spread out very thinly. However, if a supernova sends a shockwave rippling through a nebula it can compress parts of the cloud. The **denser** pockets of gas and dust may then have just enough gravity to start shrinking and pulling more material in. This is the process that gave birth to our Sun.

ABOVE: *Deep inside the Trifid Nebula, new stars are being born. Our Sun formed about 5 billion years ago in a nebula like this.*

As gas and dust was drawn into the part of the nebula that was to form our Sun, this dense pocket of debris began to spin. And as gravity made it shrink, it spun faster—just as ice skaters spin faster when they pull in their arms. The gas and dust became concentrated in a huge, spinning disk, with most of the matter in a collapsing ball of gas at its center—the young Sun.

As the young Sun got heavier, its gravity increased and it pulled in more and more material. The colliding gas **molecules** started to heat up, making the ball of gas glow weakly. All the time, the pressure and temperature in the core were getting higher until, finally, they reached a point where **nuclear fusion** could begin. Fusion spread through the core in an instant, and the Sun lit up, as if someone had turned on a cosmic light switch.

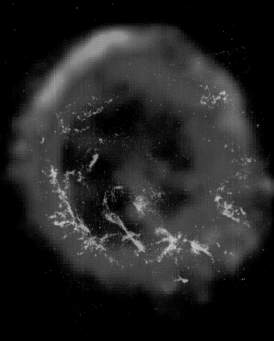

RIGHT: *The debris from a supernova forms a gas cloud called a nebula. After millions of years, the gas and dust in a nebula may get recycled into new stars.*

The Sun's Family

The newly formed Sun was surrounded by a disk of gas, ice, and dust. Over millions of years these materials began to collide and merge to form the planets and moons of the solar system.

Today we know of nine planets **orbiting** the Sun. The closest are small worlds made of rock and metal: Mercury, Venus, Earth, and Mars. Beyond Mars is the **asteroid belt,** a cloud of rubble left over after the planets had formed. Way beyond this lie the giant planets: enormous Jupiter, Saturn and its magnificent rings, Uranus, and Neptune. Unlike the inner planets, these are huge worlds made up of gas and ice. The furthest known planet is tiny Pluto, which is made mostly of ice.

Different types of planets formed in different parts of the solar system because of their distance from the Sun. Close to the Sun, the **solar wind** soon blew away gases such as **hydrogen** and **helium,** leaving behind water, dust, and solid glassy particles called **chondrules.** These materials formed the solid inner planets and Earth's large moon. Another solid world would have formed in the asteroid belt, but Jupiter's enormous **gravity** prevented the asteroids from clumping together.

The gases hydrogen and helium collected in the outer territories of the young solar system.

BELOW: *This composite photograph shows the family of planets that make up our solar system, in order (from bottom to top) of their nearness to the Sun: Mercury, Venus, Earth, Mars (known as the inner planets), Jupiter, Saturn, Uranus, Neptune (known as the gas giants), and distant and icy Pluto.*

The outer planets formed from a mixture of these gases and ice. Jupiter and Saturn formed most quickly, growing huge and pulling in vast amounts of hydrogen and helium. Uranus and Neptune formed more slowly. Most of the hydrogen and helium around them blew away before they could capture it, so these planets consist largely of ice. Tiny Pluto formed from icy **debris** at the edge of the solar system, where there was not enough material to produce giant planets.

ABOVE: *This artist's impression shows the newly formed Sun (right) surrounded by a ring of debris and a young planet (left).*

Pierre-Simon de Laplace
(1749–1827)

The first person to propose a complete theory of the birth of the Sun and solar system was French astronomer Pierre-Simon de Laplace. In 1796 he stated that the planets formed from a circular cloud around the young Sun, which separated into individual rings that later formed planets. His theory was accepted for a century before new discoveries showed it must be wrong.

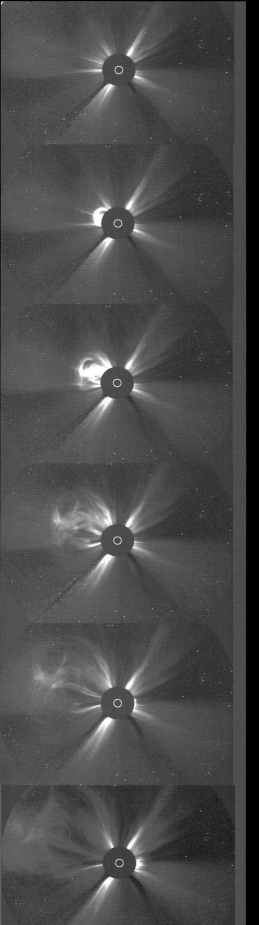

Storms on the Sun

Your **mission** is over and you're now heading home, glad to leave the fiery sunscape behind. But only a few weeks into the return journey, the Sun has one last spectacular surprise in store for you.

Alarms sound all over the ship, waking you suddenly in your darkened sleeping quarters. You rush to the bridge to see what's happening, but the Sun looks perfectly normal through the rear view window. Perhaps something is happening in the **corona,** hidden by the glare of the Sun's face. You activate the coronal viewer to block out light from the **photosphere,** and what you see next makes you gasp.

An enormous bubble is rising from the corona, expanding to an unbelievable size—bigger even than the Sun itself. The bubble seems to have formed over a cluster of **sunspots,** and your ship's instruments indicate that it contains billions of tons of **plasma.** You watch in amazement as it grows and grows until it is hundreds of times bigger than the Sun. The gigantic bubble is a Sun storm, or **coronal mass ejection.** Luckily this Sun storm isn't heading for you. Instead, it's heading straight for Earth—and at the phenomenal speed it's traveling it will get there in just two or three days.

Our planet is shielded from Sun storms and the **solar wind.** Earth's **magnetic field** deflects plasma from the Sun, capturing some of the **particles** but sending most flowing around Earth like water around an island. The captured particles whirl around inside the Earth's magnetic field, picking up speed and energy. Some of these trapped particles then crash into the upper atmosphere near the **poles.**

LEFT: *A coronal mass ejection blasts out of the Sun, forming a massive bubble of plasma. These photographs, taken by the SOHO space probe, use a coronal viewer that blocks out the Sun's glare (blue circle in middle). The Sun's position is shown by a white outline.*

As the particles collide with air **molecules,** they release energy as different colors of light, creating a fantastic multicolored light show across the night sky. These beautiful displays are called the northern lights, or **aurora** borealis, and the southern lights, or aurora australis. They usually occur near the poles, but after a large Sun storm they can spread all the way to the **equator.**

Though we are protected from the full force of Sun storms, they can still cause havoc. **Satellites** sometimes break down after Sun storms, putting telephones and TV stations out of action, and shuttle astronauts must stay on board their craft to avoid deadly bursts of solar wind. Even on the ground things can go wrong. Changes in Earth's magnetic field following a Sun storm can produce surges in power lines, causing power failures. A Sun storm in 1989 caused a massive power failure in Canada, leaving six million people without electricity.

ABOVE: *Earth's magnetic field (blue-green) protects us from the solar wind and Sun storms. The continual force of the solar wind shapes our planet's magnetic field.*

RIGHT: *The northern lights, or aurora borealis, can be brighter than moonlight. This picture was taken in Fairbanks, Alaska.*

Myths and Legends

ABOVE: *A painting on an ancient Greek bowl shows the Greek Sun god Helios driving the Sun across the sky in his chariot.*

For thousands of years before the age of science, people worshiped the Sun as a source of life and heat, and told stories to explain its origins. Although there are some prehistoric cave paintings of the Sun, it doesn't seem to have been as important to early hunters as images of magic animals and goddesses. When people began to settle down and farm crops for the first time, the Sun became much more important.

One of the oldest monuments thought to have been built by Sun-worshipers is the giant stone circle at Stonehenge in England. It was constructed between about 3000 and 2000 B.C., but no one is exactly sure why —the builders did not leave any writing behind to explain its purpose. However, it is aligned so that certain stones point to the midsummer and midwinter sunrise and sunset, so it may have been used as a calendar. It was built around the time that people in England began to lead settled lives as farmers, and calendars would have told them when to plant their crops.

BELOW: *The ancient monument of Stonehenge is believed to have been built to trace the Sun's location at sunrise and sunset on the longest and shortest days of the year. This huge calendar took its builders some 1,500 years to complete.*

Temples of the Sun

The people of Mexico and Central and South America were great Sun worshipers. Before the European invasion in about 1500 A.D., Mayans, Toltecs, Aztecs, and Incas all built temples that lined up with the rising and setting Sun at different times of year. The Aztecs especially believed the Sun was a powerful god, making mass human sacrifices during **eclipses** to make sure it returned. This Incan festival honoring the Sun god is still celebrated in Peru today.

Sun worship was also very important to the ancient Egyptians, who worshiped not one but four Sun gods. These were Aten (the Disk of the Sun), Kephri (the rising Sun), Ra (the midday Sun), and Atum (the setting Sun).

The ancient Greeks had a Sun god they called Helios, who drove the Sun across the sky in a chariot every day. The Romans turned Helios into their god Apollo, and held big festivals on midwinter's day, the shortest day of the year, to celebrate the death and rebirth of the Sun. When Rome converted to Christianity, this festival was taken over by Christmas, which is still celebrated near midwinter.

BELOW: *An Egyptian pharaoh and his family make an offering to the Sun god Aten in this ancient carving from 1365–1349 B.C.*

Early Observations

Despite all their myths and legends, the ancient Greeks and Romans were probably the first people to study the Sun scientifically. They knew that it could not really be close enough for it to have melted the wings of their legendary hero Icarus, and that it was not really drawn around the sky in a chariot.

The Greek scientist Aristarchus (c. 310–230 B.C.) was the first to realize that the Sun was much bigger and further away than the Moon. At the time, most astronomers believed that Earth was at the center of the universe, with the Sun, Moon, and planets circling it.

ABOVE: *White light from the Sun is really a mixture of different colors. When a beam of sunlight passes through a raindrop or a glass prism (top) it splits into these colors, forming a pattern of colored bands called a spectrum.*

Nicolaus Copernicus
(1473–1543)

*Polish astronomer Nicolaus Copernicus was the first to publish a convincing argument that Earth and the other planets **orbit** the Sun. Copernicus studied mathematics and astronomy in universities in Poland and Italy before he became canon (minister) of the Polish cathedral in Frauenburg. This secure job allowed him to pursue his love of astronomy. The more he observed the solar system, the more certain he became that the Sun and planets did not move around Earth, as most people believed. He published his work as* The Revolutions of the Celestial Spheres, *but died on the day he received his first copy.*

The Greeks had already measured the size of Earth accurately, and Aristarchus thought it was strange for a large object like the Sun to circle a smaller one like Earth. He was the first person to suggest that the Sun might stand still and Earth and other planets move around it, but his ideas were forgotten about for centuries.

The idea of a Sun-centered universe resurfaced in 1543, when Polish priest Nicolaus Copernicus published a book on the theory. But it was not until the early 1600s, when the invention of the telescope revolutionized astronomy, that evidence was found to support Copernicus's theory.

Astronomers used telescopes to project images of the Sun, and so discovered **sunspots** on its surface. Although Chinese and Japanese astronomers had seen sunspots before, no one in Europe had recorded them. Ancient teachings said that the Sun was a perfect, unchanging disk, but the sunspots proved them wrong—and if they were wrong about this, then they might be wrong about everything.

Astronomers continued to study sunspots and improved their measurements of the size and distance of the Sun, but ideas about its structure and the source of its enormous heat and power took longer to develop. Some people thought the Sun was a huge ball of burning coal. However, even a lump of coal the size of the Sun could only last for a few thousand years, and there was growing evidence that Earth was much older than that. Some scientists suggested that the Sun was shining from energy given out as it contracted, and this theory became popular for a while.

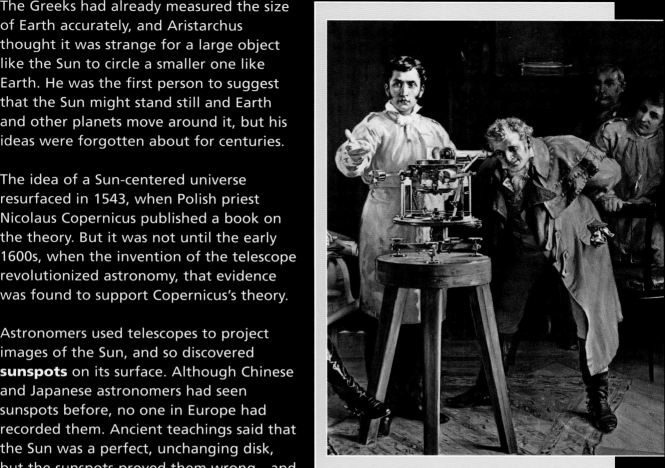

Joseph von Fraunhofer
[1787–1826]
*In 1814 the German instrument-maker Joseph von Fraunhofer was studying sunlight that had been split into colors by a prism. He noticed that there were fine lines that were blocking out certain colors. Curious, Fraunhofer found similar lines in the spectrum of light from a flame. In 1859 the German scientists Robert Bunsen and Gustav Kirchoff showed that the dark lines are caused by **atoms** of certain **elements** that absorb particular colors of light. Fraunhofer lines have now become the most important way of finding out what elements are in distant stars and planets.*

Solar Eclipses

Eclipses are simply huge shadows. A solar eclipse occurs when the Moon passes in front of the Sun and casts a shadow on Earth. Lunar eclipses happen when Earth casts a shadow on the Moon. Because of a lucky coincidence, solar eclipses give us a unique opportunity to study the Sun's **corona.** The Sun is 400 times wider than the Moon, but it is also 400 times further away. As a result, the Sun and Moon appear almost exactly the same size in the sky. During a total solar eclipse, the Moon blocks the Sun's face precisely, but leaves the fainter corona uncovered.

Total solar eclipses are rare and spectacular occasions, watched by millions of people when they happen. The Moon takes about an hour to slowly slide across the Sun's face and gradually cover it. The period when the Sun is completely blocked—called totality—lasts only a few minutes. As totality approaches the temperature falls and the sky suddenly darkens, turning day into night.

ABOVE: *The diamond ring occurs seconds before totality, when the last rays of sunlight shine around the edge of the Moon.*

BELOW: *During totality day turns to night and the Sun's vast corona becomes visible. This is the only time the corona is visible from Earth.*

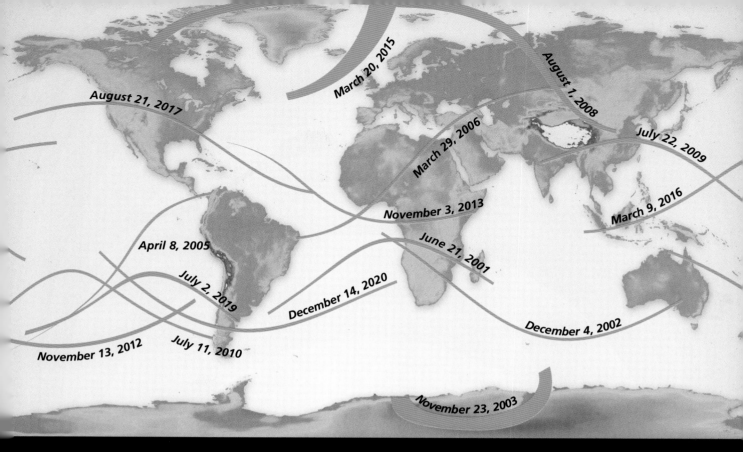

August 21, 2017

March 20, 2015

August 1, 2008

July 22, 2009

March 29, 2006

March 9, 2016

November 3, 2013

April 8, 2005

June 21, 2001

July 2, 2019

December 14, 2020

December 4, 2002

November 13, 2012

July 11, 2010

November 23, 2003

Seconds before totality, the last rays of sunlight cause the beautiful "diamond ring effect." Then the **photosphere** disappears completely and the corona appears as a magnificent halo around the Moon, with streams of **plasma** stretching far into space. Close to the edge of the Moon, tiny red **prominences** are sometimes visible.

Because the Moon's **orbit** is not a perfect circle, its size in the sky changes from time to time. Sometimes it is not quite big enough to cover the Sun completely, and it leaves a ring of sunlight visible around it. This is called an annular eclipse. When the Moon covers only one side of the Sun it causes a partial eclipse.

Solar eclipses are extraordinary events, and some people travel across the world to see them. However, they can be dangerous because they tempt people to look directly at the Sun. You should never do this without approved eye protection. The safest way to study the Sun is to project its image through a pinhole in a piece of card onto a sheet of white paper and to view its image on the paper.

ABOVE: *This map shows where total solar eclipses can be seen between the years 2000 and 2020.*

BELOW: *When the Moon covers only the middle of the Sun it produces an annular eclipse.*

Probes to the Sun

Space probes have transformed our theories about the Sun thanks to their ability to see types of solar **radiation** that are invisible to the human eye or blocked by Earth's **atmosphere.** Probes that can detect **ultraviolet light** and **X-rays** showed that the Sun glows brightly in both these radiations. Ultraviolet light and X-rays are given off only by the hottest parts of the Sun's outer layers, such as the **corona,** so they give scientists a way of studying these hot regions.

The first interplanetary probes—the Pioneer probes—confirmed the existence of the **solar wind.** *Pioneers 6, 7, 8,* and *9* **orbited** the Sun near Earth's own path, and sent back reports for many years.

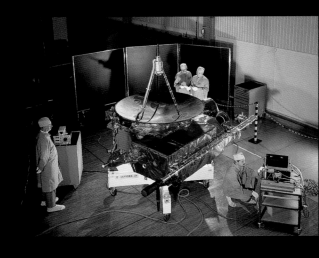

ABOVE: *Technicians carry out tests on the* Ulysses *space probe prior to its launch in October 1990.*

BELOW: *This artist's impression shows* Ulysses *shortly after its release from a space shuttle.*

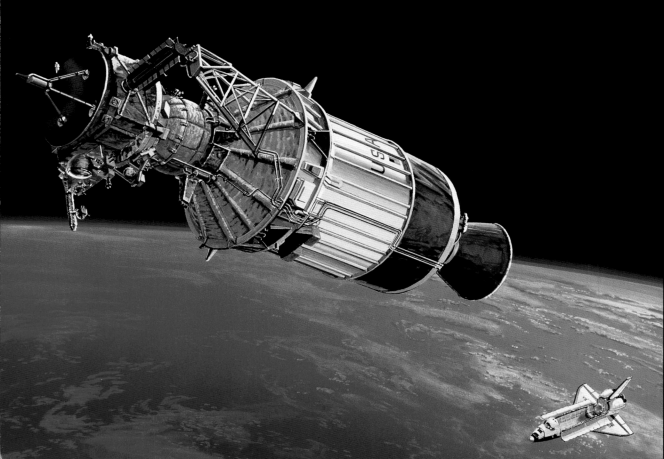

More ambitious recent **missions** have traveled closer to the Sun, observed different types of radiation, and viewed the Sun from different angles.

One of the most successful missions was *Ulysses*, a European probe launched in 1990 into an orbit that takes it high over the Sun's north and south **poles**—far above and below the plane of the solar system. *Ulysses* discovered large holes in the corona over the poles.

SOHO, the Solar and Heliospheric Observatory, is a joint European/NASA mission, launched in 1995, that orbits the Sun around 900,000 miles (1.5 million kilometers) from Earth. *SOHO* is designed to look at the Sun's corona using ultraviolet telescopes, and also to measure the rise and fall of the Sun's surface as sunquakes ripple through it.

The Ulysses *probe orbits the Sun in an unusual way. Planets orbit the Sun's* **equator**, *so they all lie in the same plane.* Ulysses *orbits the Sun's poles, which takes it outside the plane of the solar system (artist's impression).*

TRACE, the Transition Region and Coronal Explorer, was launched by NASA in 1998 to study the corona, especially the region at the base of the corona where the temperature rises dramatically relative to that of the **photosphere**. *TRACE* is also equipped with an ultraviolet telescope.

The End of the Sun

About 5 billion years in the future, the Sun will run out of **hydrogen** fuel and die. Astronomers know a great deal about the life cycle of stars because there are so many stars to study. Big stars die with a huge explosion called a **supernova,** but small stars like the Sun die in a less violent way.

As the Sun's hydrogen gets used up, the zone where fusion takes place will spread out. This change will upset the balance between the inward pull of **gravity** and the outward push of **radiation** that keeps the Sun a steady size. As outward push takes over, the Sun will swell to about 100 times wider, becoming a type of star called a **red giant.** The red giant will swallow the planets Mercury, Venus, and possibly Earth.

Eventually **nuclear fusion** will be fueled by **helium** rather than hydrogen. As a result, the Sun will shrink. But the helium will run out and the Sun will swell up again. This time there is no way back—the Sun will keep expanding, blowing away its outer layers to form a huge gas cloud called a planetary **nebula.** At the heart of the nebula the Sun's **core** will shrink into a tiny star called a **white dwarf** about the size of Earth, but so dense that a matchbox of it would weigh as much as an elephant.

The Eskimo Nebula formed when a star like our Sun died. The dying star blew out its gases into a huge cloud, lit by a tiny white dwarf star—the remains of the core—in the heart of the nebula.

The Sun's death will mean the end of life on Earth—at best, our planet will become a burned cinder **orbiting** a dead star. If our descendants are still around, they will not be living in the solar system. Perhaps technology will have advanced enough for the entire human race to pack up and leave for other colonies, scattered across the **galaxy.**

Glossary

asteroid belt ring made up of large chunks of rock called asteroids that orbit the Sun between the orbits of Mars and Jupiter

atmosphere layer of gas trapped by gravity around the surface of a planet, moon, or star

atom tiny particle of matter

aurora colorful glow in the sky seen near the poles at night, caused by plasma hitting the atmosphere

axis imaginary line through the middle of a planet that the planet spins around

chondrule fragment of material from the early solar system that heated, melted, and refroze to form a glassy particle. It is one of the materials that formed the inner planets and moons.

convective zone region below the Sun's surface where hot plasma bubbles up to the surface, releases light energy, and then sinks back down

core center of a planet, moon, or star, where the heaviest elements have collected

corona outer atmosphere of the Sun

coronal mass ejection eruption of a huge amount of plasma from the Sun's corona. It is also known as a Sun storm.

debris fragments of rock, dust, ice, or other materials floating in space

dense having a lot of weight squeezed into a small space

diameter width of an object measured by drawing a straight line through its center

eclipse effect caused by a planet or moon moving in front of the Sun, blocking it out, and casting a shadow on another object

electron negatively charged particle in the outer part of an atom

element chemical that cannot be split into any other chemicals

ellipse stretched circle, or oval

equator imaginary line around the center of a planet, midway between the poles

galaxy collection of millions of stars held together by gravity

granulation speckled pattern of dark lines around brighter areas on the Sun's surface

gravity force that pulls objects together. The heavier or closer an object is, the stronger is its pull, or gravity.

helium second most common element in the universe. Helium is also the second most common gas found in the Sun.

hemisphere top or bottom half of a planet, moon, or star

hydrogen simplest, lightest, and most common element in the universe. The Sun consists mostly of hydrogen, which is the fuel that makes stars shine.

magnetic field region around a planet where a compass can detect the north pole

mass measure of the amount of material in an object, and how it is affected by gravity

mission expedition to visit a specific target in space, such as a planet or moon

molecule tiny unit of matter consisting of two or more atoms joined together

nebula cloud of gas and dust stretching across a vast region of space

neutrino particle released in nuclear fusion

neutron uncharged particle found in the nuclei of most atoms

nuclear fusion process in which the nuclei of atoms fuse together, releasing vast amounts of energy. Sunlight is produced by nuclear fusion.

nucleus (plural is nuclei) center of an atom

orbit path an object takes around another when it is trapped by the larger object's gravity; or, to take such a path

particle tiny fragment of an atom. Particle can also mean a speck of dust or dirt.

photosphere surface of the Sun

plasma gas so hot that its atoms are torn apart into smaller particles

pole point on surface of a planet, moon, or star coinciding with the top or bottom end of its axis

prominence gigantic arch of plasma that forms over the Sun's surface

proton positively charged particle in the nucleus of an atom

radiation energy released in rays from a source. Heat and light are types of radiation.

radiative zone region surrounding the Sun's core where energy moves toward the convective zone as radiation

red giant old star that has expanded with age and turned red

rotate to turn around an object's center, or axis

satellite object that orbits a planet

solar flare sudden burst of plasma and radiation from a sunspot at the bottom of the corona

solar wind constant stream of plasma that travels out of the Sun and through the solar system at very high speed

space probe robotic vehicle sent from Earth to study the solar system

spicule short-lived jet of plasma that shoots out of the Sun's surface into its corona

sunspot dark spot on the Sun's surface where the temperature is slightly lower

supernova colossal explosion produced by the death of a large star

ultraviolet light type of invisible light given off by objects hotter or with more energy than ones that glow with blue or violet light

wavelength property of light and other forms of radiation. We see light of specific wavelengths as colors, and light of mixed wavelengths as white.

white dwarf dim, white star about the same size as Earth but much denser

X-ray type of invisible radiation, stronger than ultraviolet light, given off by extremely hot objects like the Sun

zero gravity absence of gravity in space, causing objects to become weightless and float in midair

More Books to Read

Couper, Heather, and Nigel Henbest. *The DK Space Encyclopedia.* New York: Dorling Kindersley, 1999.
Estella, Robert, and Marcel Socias. *Our Star: The Sun.* Hauppage, New York: Barrons Juveniles, 1993.
Kerrod, Robin. *The Sun.* Minneapolis, Minn.: Lerner Publications Company, 2000.
Simon, Seymour. *The Solar System.* New York: William Morrow, 1992.

Index

Picture Credits
Key: t – top, b – below, c – center, l – left, r – right. **AURA/NOAO/NSF**: 14b, 17, T. Rimmele, M. Hanna 15t; **European Southern Observatory**: 22; **NASA**: 4–5b, 7b, CXC/SAO/HST/ATNF/ATCA 23b, A. Fruchter/ERO 36, Jeff Hester (Arizona State Univ.) 23t, Marshall Space Flight Center 11t, 15b; **TRACE**: 11b; **SOHO***: 3, 4l, 7, 10, 12t, 12b, 13t, 20–21t, 26, 27t; **Corbis**: Gianni Dagli Orti 29cr, Araldo de Luca 28t, Ric Ergenbright 29t, Roger Ressmeyer 28–29b; **Hulton Getty**: 31; **Image Bank**: Marc Romanelli 8–9; **Mary Evans Picture Library**: 21b; **Science Photo Library**: 13bl, 13bc, 13br, 24, 30cr, Boeing/NASA 2, 34b, John Bova 14t, Chris Butler 25t, Jean-Loup Charmet 25b, Dr Fred Espenak 32b, European Space Agency 34t, Jack Finch 27b, Tommaso Guicciardini/INFN 19cr, Ton Kinsbergen/ESA 35, Los Alamos National Laboratory 18b, David Nunuk 32t, David Parker 30t, Pekka Parviainen 9, George Post 1, 33b, US Library of Congress 18t. Front cover: SoHO. Back cover: NASA, JPL/California Institute of Technology.
*SOHO is a project of international cooperation between ESA & NASA.